100 Favourite
After-Dinner
Stories *from*
The Famous

100 Favourite After-Dinner Stories *from* The Famous

Collected
by
PHYLLIS
SHINDLER

LONDON   NEW YORK   SYDNEY   TORONTO

This edition published in 1993
by BCA by arrangement with
Judy Piatkus (Publishers) Ltd, London W1

CN 4431

Printed in Great Britain

This is my fourth collection of stories and anecdotes from distinguished people.

The royalties will be devoted to Ravenswood, which cares for mentally handicapped children and those with learning difficulties.

I hope this book will give pleasure to the reader and will also be of use to the potential after-dinner speaker.

My thanks to all those who cared enough to contribute to this compilation.

Phyllis Shindler

Contributors

8

Foreword
by The Rt. Hon. The Lord Mayor of London
Sir Francis McWilliams, G.B.E., B.Sc., F.Eng., D.C.L.

I gladly welcome Phyllis Shindler's fourth book of jokes, stories and anecdotes culled from those in and around public life.

Her previous collections have brought much life and laughter to many sombre sessions, and have raised many thousands of pounds for some excellent charitable causes.

The new offering will, I am sure, attract a large number of people, lots of whom will use it as a tool of their trade and encourage others to do likewise.

All the royalties will be donated by Mrs Shindler to Ravenswood, which is devoted to the care of mentally handicapped children, and those who have learning difficulties.

9

Evelyn Anthony
Best-selling Author

A Catholic, a Protestant and a Jew were asked when they thought life began. The Catholic said, 'On conception.' The Protestant said, 'At birth.' The Jew said, 'When the dog dies and the kids leave home!'

Dr Mary Archer

M.A., Ph.D, F.R.S.C.

Chemist, Lecturer, Writer and
Business Executive

When my two boys were quite small, we had a lady to
stay with us whom I shall refer to as Mrs Smith.

Now Mrs Smith was fond of the odd gin and tonic, and
I was not quite sure how my boys and she would get on.
So I told them they must be very polite to her, even if her
behaviour appeared a little strange.

And, to do them justice, they were extremely polite to
Mrs Smith. They helped her unpack when she arrived,
and they showed her round the garden – although it was
raining at the time.

Then, when it came to teatime, my elder son Will
asked Mrs Smith if he might sit next to her.

'Of course you can, William,' she said. 'But why do
you want to sit next to me?'

'Well,' said Will, 'I want to watch you drink your tea.'

'What a funny little boy,' replied Mrs Smith. 'Why do
you want to watch me drink my tea?'

'Well,' replied Will, 'last night I heard my Mummy tell
my Daddy that you can drink like a fish.'

The Rt. Hon. Lord Justice Balcombe
Lord Justice of Appeal
Writer

I was newly appointed to the High Court bench which, as most people know, meant that my earnings were substantially below those which I had received at the Bar. I was sitting in Liverpool, hearing an application by a divorced wife for an increase in the periodical payments made to her by her ex-husband. The husband's case was that he had been promoted within his firm from a blue collar to a white collar job, which meant that his take-home pay was less than it had been as he no longer had the opportunity to earn overtime. He was asked by the wife's counsel:

'How can you say that you have been promoted when your pay is less than it was before your so-called promotion?'

At which the husband's counsel, in an aside which I was obviously intended to hear, said: 'I wouldn't make that point in front of his Lordship if I were you.'

Lynne Reid Banks
Writer

My very best after-dinner story cannot be of any use to anyone else, especially to men. It is a perfectly true story but not, I imagine, one that anyone would want to adopt because no-one would want to admit to looking such a complete dork.

It happened in 1959 when I was travelling from Paris to the South of France in a couchette. This rather luxurious mode of travel was not what I was accustomed to (ITN was paying) and I was enchanted by all the little home comforts in my tiny sleeping compartment: a minute washbasin built into a little rounded corner cupboard which, when opened, proved to contain a splendid jerry. I hadn't used one of these since childhood, but for some reason – perhaps the length of the train corridor and my lack of a dressing gown – I decided to use this one prior to turning in. So, clad in the sweet simplicity of a knee-length nightie, I lowered myself on to the pot.

At this moment, the train rounded a bend. Off-balance and having nothing to hold on to, I gripped the rim of my throne, which skidded forward with the giddy motion of the train. To my horror, the folding doors that divided my couchette from the next were improperly fastened and now flew open, just as momentum projected me, on my jerry, into the room next door!

I retain a searing memory of a heavily moustached French face peering in drop-jawed amazement from his bunk, before the train swung round a reverse curve. The motion of this sent me hurtling backwards, the way I had come. The folding doors closed after me, leaving my neighbour, no doubt, wondering if he had dreamt the strange apparition of a woman on a po sailing into and out of his compartment in a matter of seconds!

Of course, being French, perhaps he was better able to reconcile himself to such odd occurrences than I was. It goes without saying that I have never been able to so much as look at a jerry since!

Margaret Beckett
M.P.
Deputy Leader of the Labour Party, 1992–

On safari

In 1974, between the elections, I was Judith Hart's
political adviser at Overseas Development and travelled
with her to Tanzania. Towards the end of our stay, we
spent an afternoon in the Lake Manyara park – a
fascinating experience considerably enlivened by a brief
encounter with a 'guard' elephant escorting a party of
calves.

Although the elephant advanced on our Land Rover in
an extremely menacing fashion, I was sure that I was
foolish to be alarmed – after all, the Head of the regional
Government was with us and presumably they wouldn't
let anything happen to him! In fact, all the old Africa
hands in the party told us at the end of the day that we
had actually been in real and very great danger. Judith
turned to her Private Secretary, who had been travelling
near the end of the convoy, and asked why he hadn't
come rushing up to save her. 'Oh, no, Minister,' he
replied sweetly, 'you quite misunderstand the role of the
Private Secretary. It's my job to go back and tell the
Department what happened to you.'

The Rt. Hon. Tony Benn

M.P.

Politician

In 1956 I attended a meeting in Taunton to speak at the by-election. It was a crowded eve of poll meeting and the Labour candidate was called Reg Pestell – now Lord Wells-Pestell.

After I had spoken, the Chairman got up to introduce the candidate and he did it in this way:

'And now, Comrades, I want to introduce to you Mr Reg Pestell, the Labour candidate for Taunton, who on Thursday, we are all confident, will strike a powerful blow *at* Great Britain and the interests of its people.'

As so often happens at rallies of this kind, nobody batted an eyelid and Reg Pastell rose to a thunder of applause, perhaps not even having noticed himself what had been said.

Sir Isaiah Berlin

O.M., C.B.E.
Philosopher and Writer

In Birmingham, the famous architect, Sir Edwin Lutyens, was to make a speech, presided over by the Lord Mayor of Birmingham. The Lord Mayor talked for something over half-an-hour, after which Lutyens got up (having been invited by the Lord Mayor to do so), looking rather cross, and said 'Any questions?'

Baroness Blackstone of Stoke Newington in Greater London

Master of Birkbeck College, Author

One little story I have occasionally told, suitably embroidered, is as follows:

An American visitor to England was very puzzled to discover that no-one in the village in which he was staying would speak to anyone in the neighbouring village. On investigating this, he found that the reason for this odd behaviour was that the neighbouring village had, several centuries earlier, failed to inform the inhabitants of the village where he was staying that the Danes were coming.

Tony Blair

M.P.

Shadow Home Secretary, 1993–

Politics – a weighty business

One of the funniest moments of my political career occurred during the election campaign in March 1992.

The Campaigns Unit at Walworth Road had arranged for me to visit the Rowntree factory in York, along with the local candidate. I was to address a lunchtime meeting of factory workers, followed by a quick question and answer session, before we were whisked off to the next engagement in Leeds.

That day I had a television crew following my progress, making a programme about what it was like on the campaign trail, to be shown after the election. The morning had been chaotic, as a result of which we arrived at the factory slightly late. My campaign aide had been concerned about this visit all along. There had not been sufficient information in advance, and we were not quite clear about where to go when we arrived. However, it was explained that the morning shift was just about to finish and that more people would probably turn up then. In the meantime, refreshments were laid on in the adjoining room. The mention of refreshments – a rare treat on the campaign trail – was enough to start a stampede next door.

The room was comfortably laid out, with soft sofas grouped round coffee tables. The camera crew at once decided that this would be a much better room for their film and suggested that we move the meeting through there instead. No-one objected, so my aide went back and forth to the other room and brought the audience through. Eventually there were about a dozen people gathered, and it was getting a bit crowded on the sofa. We'd drunk the coffee and circulated the chocolate biscuits – although the Rowntree people didn't seem too keen on the latter – and we decided it was time to start the meeting.

My aide went off to see if anyone was left next door. A few moments later she returned, in what I could see was a state of great amusement. However, I was deep in conversation and the cameras were rolling, so I did not find out until later what had reduced her to near hysterical hilarity.

Apparently, when she went back, the big room had greatly filled up and a woman was setting up chairs on the stage. My aide had gone up to her, introduced herself, and said that we had moved the meeting next door. A blank stare had been the only reply. She tried again. More blank looks.

Finally, the woman on the stage had said:

'I think we are at cross-purposes here. I don't know what you mean. This is the Weight-Watchers meeting.'

Professor Margaret A Boden

F.B.A., M.A., Sc.D. (Cantab), Ph.D. (Harvard)
Professor of Philosophy and Psychology

An American Nobel prizewinner in Physics was giving his acceptance speech in Stockholm. He described how, a couple of months before, he and his wife had been driving through the Arizona desert. They came to a scruffy, run-down petrol station in the middle of the desert and stopped for petrol.

The attendant came out to help them – a lank and dirty man in filthy overalls and broken shoes. When the wife saw the man, she jumped out of the car and flung herself into his arms. They embraced passionately while her husband filled up the car himself. (He said nothing, as he could not trust himself to speak).

When they drove off, his wife blowing kisses to the man left behind, her husband asked for an explanation. She told him that she had known the man when they were both students. Indeed, they had nearly got married.

'Ah! How different your life would have been if you'd married him,' said the physicist.

'Oh, I don't know,' she replied. 'If I'd married him, perhaps *he* would have won the Nobel Prize.'

Professor Sir Hermann Bondi

K.C.B., F.R.S., F.R.A.S.
Fellow of Churchill College, Cambridge

A story from school: The English class is covering *The Merchant of Venice* when, due to illness of the English teacher, a substitute teacher from another subject has to take a lesson. During this, they come to the line 'The quality of mercy is not strained.' One of the children asks this teacher whether the word 'strained' has the meaning of 'stretched' or 'filtered'. The substitute teacher hums and haws for a while and then remarks, 'As it says 'not strained' it does not matter which.'

The Rt. Hon. Lord Boyd-Carpenter

D.L.

Politician and Author

When Lord Birkenhead, then F.E. Smith, was a youngish barrister, he had a row with a very pompous judge. This culminated in the judge saying to him, 'You are offensive, Mr Smith,' to which F.E. Smith replied, 'Yes, Your Honour, we both are, but the difference is I am trying to be and you cannot help it.'

Lord Brabourne
Film and Television Producer

At the end of a very long City dinner, at which there had been too many speeches, the Master of Ceremonies called upon the Guest of Honour to 'give his Address.'

The Speaker then rose hastily to his feet and said, 'Ladies and Gentlemen, I am delighted to give you my Address, which is Number 41, Hyde Park Corner, to which I am now returning!' After this he left the room to a stunned silence, followed by loud applause.

Richard Branson
Founder and Chairman of the
Virgin Group of Companies
Philanthropist

The other week we had a lovely old lady flying with us in Upper Class. Our hostess asked what was in the box she was carrying on board, and was told it was her dog. She politely told the lady that dogs were not allowed in Upper Class and had the box stowed away.

On arriving at JFK airport, the hostess looked into the box to find, to her horror, that the dog was dead. Our Head of Ground Operations took charge. He sent the hostess home and told her he'd deliver the dog to the lady the following day – free of charge.

He then headed off to the nearest pet shop, found another dog that looked nearly identical and took him round to the lady's house. When the lady opened the door, rather than a joyous reunion, she looked at the dog and said, *'That's* not *my* dog – *my* dog is dead!'

Moyra Bremner
Best-selling Author and Broadcaster
Professional Speaker and Chairwoman

I've been experimenting with making wine and, frankly, I'm rather proud of my latest vintage. In fact I rather fancy myself as a wine maker, so when my father-in-law called round I thought I'd surprise him with a glassful. He took a mouthful and asked where it had been made.

I said 'In the kitchen.'

'Doesn't travel well, does it?' he said.

Sir Robin Butler

G.C.B., C.V.O.

Secretary of the Cabinet and Head of the Home Civil
Service

A man approached the Pearly Gates and was asked by St
Peter whether he had ever done anything wrong.

'I was a rugby referee,' said the man, 'and when I was
refereeing an international match between Wales and
England at Cardiff Arms Park, I wrongly awarded a try to
England when one of their players had committed an
infringement.'

'That doesn't sound too bad,' said St Peter, 'if that is all
you have done. How long ago did this happen?'

'About 30 seconds ago,' said the man.

Peter Cadbury

Chairman of the George Cadbury Trust
Philanthropist
Industrialist

Some years ago I gave a lecture on test piloting to Her
Majesty's Guests at Pentonville prison. Shortly after that
I read a paper on the same subject to a very distinguished
society, The Sette of Odd Volumes. I apologised in
advance to the society members who may have heard my
lecture on the previous occasion.

*   *   *

They always used to say that when a lawyer sees a rift in
the lute, he widens the rift and collects the loot.

29

Sir Hugh Casson

C.H., K.C.V.O., R.A.

Past President of the Royal Academy
Author

A schoolboy enters a class late.
   'You should have been here at nine o'clock, Thompson.' Thompson replies: 'Why, what happened?'

The Rt. Hon. Lord Charteris of Amisfield

G.C.B., K.C.B., G.C.V.O.

Provost of Eton 1978–91

At a private school, a master was giving a lecture on Biology, in which he said, 'A single rabbit can reproduce itself 500 times a year.'

A small boy, raising his hand, asked, 'Please, sir, how many times can a married rabbit reproduce itself?'

The Rt. Hon. Lord Cledwyn of Penrhos

C.H.

Leader of the Opposition, House of Lords, 1982–92

The Archbishop of Canterbury was preaching his first sermon at the Temple Church. As he ascended to the pulpit, the verger said, 'Please speak up clearly, my Lord Archbishop. The agnostics are terrible here.'

The Rt. Hon. Lord Colnbrook

K.C.M.G.

Politician

Field Marshal Montgomery was well known to be a passionate opponent of both smoking and drinking, and frequently used to harangue his troops on the subject. One evening he did so in an after-dinner speech to the officers of one of the divisions under his command. He was followed by the author and MP, A.P. Herbert, who said:

'I want to tell you about my father. He always got up late and had a glass of beer for his breakfast. After lunch, with half a bottle of wine and a cigar, he had a nap. In the evening he had two large whiskies, another half bottle of wine with his dinner and a cigar and brandy afterwards. He lived to be 93 and I can tell you, Field Marshal, that even after he had been dead for two days, he looked a lot better than you do now.'

*   *   *

A young mouse looked out of his hole one day, sniffed and smelt cheese. He was about to run out and eat it, when he remembered that his father had told him always to be very careful before going to a piece of cheese. So he sat still and listened. He heard a faint 'Miaow' and ran back inside, congratulating himself on following his father's advice.

The next day he looked out again, smelt the cheese and listened. He heard a faint 'Woof, Woof,' and said to himself, 'The dog has chased the cat away and I'm quite safe.' So he ran out and started eating the cheese. He was immediately pounced on by the cat who gobbled him up and, when he had finished, said, 'I'm so glad I followed my father's advice and learned a second language.'

Shirley Conran
Writer

The last time I was in Australia (4 March 1992) a
journalist told me that the following Sunday was
Mother's Day. I asked her when Father's Day was, and
she said, 'The rest of the year.'

Sir Colin Cowdrey

C.B.E.
Chairman of the International Cricket Council
Author

Picture, if you will, the 'well-to-do' lady who has to drive
long distances every day up and down the motorway,
but she is lucky enough to own a Rolls Royce which
makes driving easier. In fact, the driving becomes so
simple (almost boring) that she holds the wheel with one
little finger and proceeds to knit.

On one of the traffic-free days, the speed moves up to
90 miles an hour without her realising it, and inevitably a
police car comes up alongside, sirens blazing, window
down. Rather reluctantly she winds her window down,
reducing her speed marginally. The policeman shouts at
the top of his voice, 'PULL OVER'.

She shouts back, 'No, SOCKS'.

The Rt. Hon. Sir Zelman Cowen

A.K., G.C.M.G., G.C.V.O., Q.C., D.C.L.

Distinguished Lawyer and Writer

A mother was walking along a splendid golden beach on a still, sunny day. She carried her infant in her arms. Then, out at sea, a wave formed in the stillness. It grew and grew and finally it engulfed her. When it receded, she saw to her horror that the babe had been taken and carried out to sea.

She was distraught. She looked up at the heavens. 'Dear God,' she said, 'what have you done? Please, please, bring back my baby.'

Nothing happened for perhaps ten minutes. Then, in the stillness, a second wave formed. It rose and rose and, once again, it engulfed her. As it withdrew, she saw at her feet the baby, seemingly unaffected and unhurt. She clasped it to her, full of joy.

Once again she looked to the heavens. 'Dear God,' she said, 'thank you, thank you for bringing back my child. Why you took him in the first place I don't know, but thank you for restoring him to me.'

'But,' she said, looking down at the child, 'he was wearing a hat.'

Sir Robin Day
Television and Radio Journalist
Writer

This is a true story of the very well-known man, a somewhat eccentric peer of the realm, who went into Hatchards, the famous bookshop in Piccadilly, and asked, 'Why is my book on Humility not displayed in the window?'

The Rt. Hon. Baron Deedes of Aldington

M.C., D.L.

Journalist
Politician

A young man was staying in one of the great country houses, ornate and old-fashioned. His enormous and heavily furnished bedroom included a four-poster bed. In the middle of the night, feeling the call of nature, he rose from his bed and groped his way round the room looking for the light switch, knocking over several objects as he did so. Eventually he found the door, crept down a dark corridor, found the loo and returned to bed.

Next morning, on preparing to descend for breakfast, he saw with horror that while looking for the light switch, he had knocked over an inkstand in his bedroom and his passage to the loo was marked by inky fingerprints on the rich, cream wallpaper. He took a quick decision, picked up his bag, went down to the stables, collected his car and drove away.

Some years later, he found himself back in the same neighbourhood. The earlier episode had long been on his conscience. He decided to make a call and put matters right. He gave his name to the butler, who said that her ladyship was talking with the head gardener, but if the visitor would take a seat in the hall he would inform her of his presence. The butler went off. The man, now mildly apprehensive of how the interview would go, sat down heavily in one of the chairs.

After a moment or two, he felt a faint, uneasy movement beneath him. He leapt to his feet, to discover that he had sat upon and suffocated her ladyship's small but beloved dog. He made immediately for the front door, got into his car and drove rapidly away.

Col. Rt. Hon. Sir Edward du Cann

K.B.E.

Politician
Writer

Said the after-dinner speaker, obviously well pleased
with the hospitality he had enjoyed:
   'Thank you for entertaining me so well – so different
from a dinner I attended last week. Then the chief toast
was to absent friends – coupled with the name of the
wine waiter.'

*   *   *

Advice to an after-dinner speaker:
   Do not make a Rolls Royce of a speech.
   And what do I mean by that?
   One that is hardly available, clearly well lubricated,
and seems as if it will run for ever.

Paul Eddington

C.B.E.

Actor

A traditional way for Shakespearian actors to get themselves out of a difficulty is to stop, look thoughtful and say, 'But more of this anon', make an exit and leave their colleagues to pick up the pieces!

Professor Sir Victor Elyan

Professor of Law
Writer

After speaking for a not inconsiderable period, the speaker stops to look at his wristwatch and apologises for not having taken it with him.

Whereupon a voice from the listeners is heard to say, loudly:

'That's all right. There is a *calendar* on the wall behind you!'

The Dean of Exeter
The Very Reverend R.M.S. Eyre

The vicar of a small town had a wife who was extremely inquisitive and somewhat prudish. She always inspected his desk diary to see what he was doing.

On one occasion he was invited by the Head Mistress of a local girls' school to go and talk on sex to the sixth form. He carefully wrote down in his diary under the appropriate date, 'Talk to sixth form at St Bridget's on Sailing.'

After he had fulfilled the engagement, the Head Mistress encountered his wife in the High Street and said, 'Your husband gave a really marvellous talk to our girls and it was very greatly appreciated.'

'Nonsense,' replied his wife, 'he has only done it twice: the first time he was sick and the second time his hat fell off.'

Michael Fabricant

M.P.

Member of Parliament for Mid-Staffordshire

As a 'new boy', I was delighted to be chosen to serve as Deputy Chairman of the Conservative Parliamentary Media Committee. We work alongside the Department of National Heritage and review the activities of the Press, radio and television.

Then, along came 'Red Hot Dutch', a satellite pornographic TV channel that broadcasts in the early hours. We decided to invite the Independent Television Commission, the Government Agency that controls all non-BBC television in Britain, to talk to us about it.

They announced they were going to bring along a video and show the Committee 'highlights'(?) of Red Hot Dutch's transmissions, which are beamed up from Denmark and so are beyond the aegis of the ITC.

Normally, only half a dozen MPs and Conservative Peers from 'the other place' will attend our meetings. Not this time!

We knew something was up when, about an hour before the meeting was due to commence, a strange noise could be heard in the Palace of Westminster. It was the scrape, scrape, scrape of zimmer frames as elderly Lords began to shuffle across from their side of the Palace of Westminster to ours, and soon the ancient Committee Room was packed with MPs and Peers.

After a few introductory remarks from a sombre Chief Executive of the ITC, the lights were dimmed. You could have heard a pin drop. The tape began.

It was as explicit as Members feared – or hoped for – and embarrassing to watch. Some Committee Members sat with eyes glued to the screen, others coughed, straightened their ties or fiddled in their handbags (women Members, that is); the rest (including me) watched the other MPs for their reactions.

44

Meanwhile, most of the Parliamentary Press Gallery had gathered outside the Committee Room to interview Members as they left. Unfortunately, the volume had been turned up too loud and every time the loud rhythmic groaning was punctuated by yells of pleasure, it was followed by gales of laughter from the journalists outside.

I sat there in the dark thinking how incongruous it all was in this ancient Committee Room . . .

Suddenly, the door opened. A myopic new MP appeared just as the screen was filled with . . . Well, *in flagrante!* He peered round nervously, wondering why all these MPs and Lords were sitting there in the darkness. Then his eyes settled on the TV screen in the far corner. 'Oh my God!' he cried, as he scuttled out backwards from the meeting.

Later, he told me that he was heading for a meeting of the Agricultural Committee and thought he had stumbled into some modern day Hell Fire Club . . .

Lord Fanshawe of Richmond

K.C.M.G

Mr Brezhnev, former General Secretary of the Communist Party, decided to visit a remote part of the Soviet Union in order to enjoy his favourite sport of shooting bear.

A message was sent to the local secretary of the Communist Party to inform him of Mr Brezhnev's arrival and of the necessity to provide a bear for him to shoot.

The local secretary was greatly confused as there were no bears in his district, but he wished to ingratiate himself with Mr Brezhnev and was also too frightened to inform the General Secretary that he could not carry out bear shooting in his area. He therefore sent a message welcoming Mr Brezhnev and set about looking for a bear. He found one in the local circus.

The bear was duly taken to the middle of the forest and placed on a track a mile and a half from where Mr Brezhnev would be standing with his rifle. The bear was then pushed off along the path in the general direction of Mr Brezhnev. Two minutes later a woodman was bicycling home along the track when, much to his astonishment, as he knew there were no bears in the area, he was confronted by the circus bear. The woodman was amazed, fell off his bicycle with surprise and ran off into the forest.

The bear was not put out. He picked up the bicycle – because, of course, he was a performing bear – and rode off along the path towards Mr Brezhnev. Ten minutes later Mr Brezhnev, with his rifle cocked, was astounded to see the bear cycling along and was so surprised that his rifle went off and he shot himself in the foot.

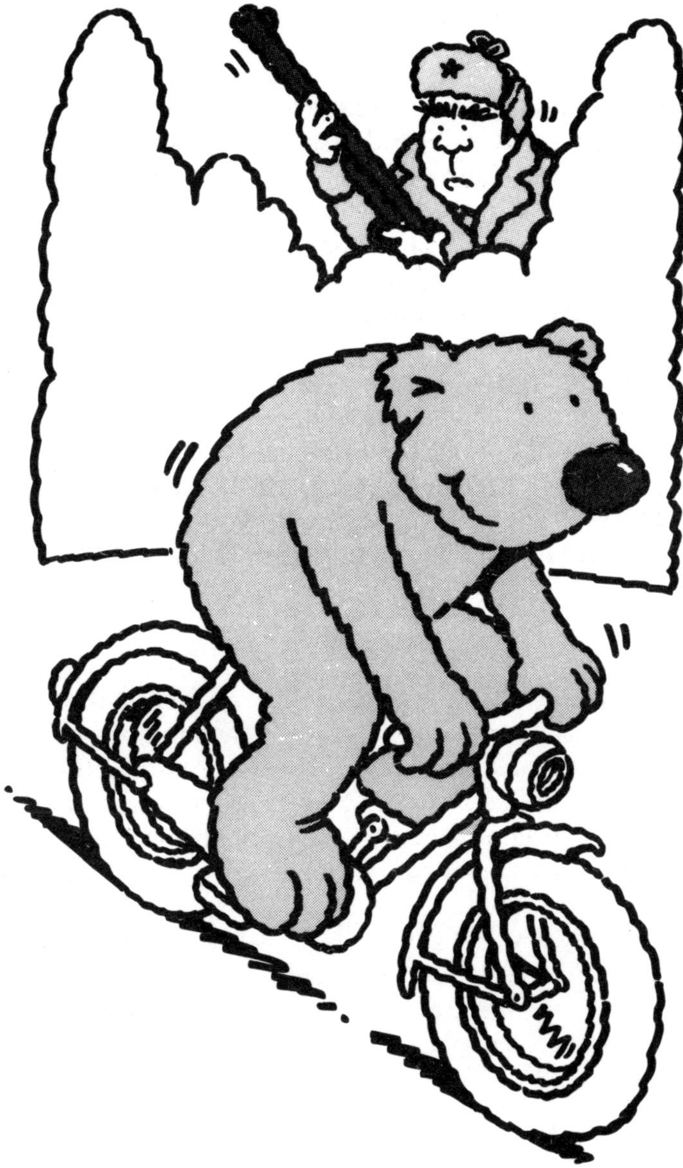

Derek Fowlds
Actor

The first and only time I made an after-dinner speech was in Australia in 1988. I was asked to speak to the National Press Club in Canberra. I made many excuses to get out of it, as I believe actors are terrible after-dinner speakers. Personally, I'm hopeless without a script and a character to hide behind. Actors who play so many different parts often don't know what to do as themselves.

After the dinner, the time came for me to speak. The Chairman rose and said how happy they were to have as their guest of honour the Principal Private Secretary to the Prime Minister in England, Mr Bernard Woolley, and he then sat down. I was stunned. Not only did I not know who I was! They didn't seem to know either!

Christina Foyle

Managing Director of W&G Foyle Ltd
Author

Coming back by ship from New York, an American got into conversation with me and said, 'My! I am looking forward to seeing your country. Do you know, I am related to Duke Ellington.' 'Really?' I replied. 'We heard him play in Harlem in New York.' He turned to me with dignity – 'I said, The Duke of Wellington!'

*   *   *

I was walking with a publisher friend down Shaftesbury Avenue, when we were stopped by a man and his wife, obviously American tourists, who asked if we could direct them to Trafalgar Square. After telling them the way, I said, 'When you get there you will see a large column with a figure on top and this is the statue of our most famous national hero, Nelson. It is called 'Nelson's Column' and he won the Battle of Waterloo.' The friend I was with said, 'And if you leave Trafalgar Square and go up the Charing Cross Road and carry straight on past Cambridge Circus, there you will see a great bookshop and this bookshop belongs to this lady.'

At this point the Americans eyed each other and the husband said, 'I get it – let's scram!'

They were just waiting for the soft touch.

John Francome

M.B.E.
Retired Champion Jockey
Author

My favourite after-dinner story concerns 'Nobby Styles', the main defender for England in the 1966 World Cup.

In the dressing room before the match against Portugal, Sir Alf Ramsey, knowing that Nobby had a reputation for being a hard tackler, said to him, 'They've only got one good player, and that's Eusebio. So Nobby, I'd like you to take him out of the game.'

Nobby replied, 'What, for this game – or forever?'

Graham Gooch

C.B.E.

Captain of the England Test Team
Author

This is a true story which I have related to many an audience on my travels around the country, speaking at cricket functions of my experiences on the international circuit.

When I first started to play for England our opponents were New Zealand, and their star bowler was Richard Hadlee – now Sir Richard Hadlee. It was at Lords cricket ground on a bright, sunny morning. England had won the toss and Mike Brearley, the Captain, decided to bat first. So 11 am arrived. The umpires and the New Zealand team were out on the field, as I walked out on to the hallowed turf with England's premier batsman, one Geoffrey Boycott. I'd barely walked two yards on to the green when Geoff said, 'Good morning.' Right away I thought, "The great man has spoken, that's a good start." We reached the wicket, and it soon became apparent that I was to take the first ball, the bowler being one of the world's best fast bowlers – Richard Hadlee. Now Richard was bowling from the Pavilion end and, to anybody who knows the Lords ground, the pitch slopes away to the right, thereby helping Hadlee's in-swinger.

To cut a long story short, I managed to survive his opening orders – while Geoff dealt capably with the other bowler, Richard Colinge – a lumbering giant of a man who did not enjoy the reputation of R. Hadlee. Anyway, I noticed that I seemed to be stuck at the end at which Hadlee was bowling. But finally I managed to snick one ball off my bat down to fine leg, whereby I ambled up to the other end for an easy single run. However, Geoff had other ideas, because he called for 'two' and I just managed to scramble home for the second run. This meant I was down Hadlee's end again, till finally I was out LBW bowled Hadlee.

As I trudged slowly back to the Pavilion, I passed Geoffrey and casually asked him the best way to play fast bowling, to which he replied, 'Always from the non-striker's end, my son.'

Lord Goodman

C.H., M.A., L.L.M.

Solicitor

Philanthropist

A man received a letter requesting him to call on his Bank Manager to discuss his overdraft. He called one day, and was given the sad news that the Bank Manager was dead. He called again the next day, again enquiring of the Bank Manager, and the sad news was confirmed.

However, he called on a third occasion to ask to speak to the Bank Manager and was told, rather impatiently, that he had already been informed on two previous occasions and why did he go on asking?

To which the man replied, 'I like to hear it.'

Rolf Harris
Television Personality

Good story . . . Small farmer from the UK migrates to Australia and starts a similar-sized sheep farm there. He eventually becomes a naturalised Australian citizen and thinks, 'I'm Australian now, so I could do it the way the Aussies do it!'

He phones up a big shearing contractor and says, 'I'd like you to send some chappies out to shear my sheep.'

The voice on the other end of the phone (a very Australian voice) says, 'Yeah, well we're in a bit of strife at the moment. The 'A' Team, that's the 24 man team, are out on the Riverina. They've got another 22 thousand to shear, so they'll be a couple of weeks yet, and the 'B' team, the 19 man team, are on the Darling Downs with 13 thousand still to shear, so . . . er . . . how many sheep have you got?'

'42!'

'Thousand?'

'No . . . individual sheep, do you see.'

There's a long silence, and eventually the man says, with a break in his voice, '. . . can I have their names?'

Admiral of the Fleet The Lord Hill-Norton

G.C.B., K.C.B.

The Virtuous Man

I am described by my friends as an exemplary man. I do not drink, seldom smoke, do not go around with women. I go to bed early and get up early. I work long hours and take exercise regularly every day. I get no financial reward for this self-denial.

All this is going to change when I get out of prison.

*   *   *

Those of us who speak Spanish will recall the old Castilian saying that an after-dinner speech is like the horns of the torero – with a point here . . . and a point there . . . and an awful lot of bull in between . . .

The Rt. Hon. Lord Holderness

Chairman, Disablement Services Authority, 1987–91

An MP, speaking at great length at his Association's
Annual General Meeting, was in full flow with the
words, '. . . not that I have particular experience of this
subject,' when a voice from the back chirped up with,
'Lack of experience never stopped a politician from
speaking about anything!'

Lady Holland-Martin

D.B.E., D.L.

Chairman, National Society for the Prevention of Cruelty
to Children, 1969–87

Child (after her first sex lesson at school):
        'Mummy, do you and daddy have sex
        relations?'
Mother: 'Well, darling, yes we do.'
Child: 'Then why haven't I met any?'

*   *   *

My Grandson (on the telephone):
        'I've got Good News and Bad News.'
Grandma: 'Let's have the Good News.'
Grandson: 'I've lost my front tooth.'
Grandma: 'Now the Bad News.'
Grandson: 'The same, Grandma, because I know you
        will be sad.'

*   *   *

Harry: 'Grandma, I have decided not to learn
        French.'
Grandma: 'I don't think Mama will be best pleased.'
Harry (shrugging his shoulders):
        'Grandma, it is pointless; I'm English!'

Bob Holness
Broadcaster and Television Presenter

An elderly lady was going down in a lift in an hotel in New York when it stopped at one of the floors. When the doors opened, three men got in. One she thought was vaguely familiar, but the other two she wasn't at all impressed by: large and grim-looking. One of them muttered to her sharply, 'Hit the ground, Grandma!' Being in New York, she did her best to fall flat on the floor . . . whereupon the three men burst out laughing. They helped her up and explained that because she was nearest to the lift buttons all they wanted her to do was to 'hit' the button marked 'Ground.' They dusted her down and she went on her way, a little shaky. That evening, she went to check out of the hotel . . . to find that her bill had been paid in full! However, there was a note for her which, when she opened it up, read, 'Sorry to have scared you: hope this makes up for it.' The signature was that of the film actor, Eddie Murphy.

Glenda Jackson

C.B.E., M.P.

Actress and Politician

Tallulah Bankhead came out of the theatre to find a
Salvation Army group with tambourines. Throwing some
money, she said, 'Here you are, darlings . . . it's been a
terrible season for you gypsy dancers.'

Elizabeth Jenkins

O.B.E.

Author and Biographer

Herbert Beerbohm Tree accepted *Pygmalion* for production at His Majesty's Theatre, with himself in the lead as Professor Higgins and Mrs Patrick Campbell as Eliza Doolittle. This was, of course, a great coup for Shaw, but the latter disliked Tree's manner of acting, as being too flamboyant.

Shaw attended the rehearsals and kept interpolating criticisms and advice until, on one occasion, Tree said: 'Mr Shaw, I cannot rehearse with you making these perpetual interruptions. I must ask you, please, to leave my theatre!'

Shaw thereupon collected his belongings and went out. When he was safely gone, Tree began working up to a tremendous bravura. Suddenly, from the dark auditorium a voice was heard, calling, 'Stop! I've come back for my umbrella.'

The Hon. Sir Asher Joel

K.B.E., O.B.E., A.O.

Australian Philanthropist, Author

If you can't judge a book by its cover then you certainly can't take for granted good conduct by an otherwise well-trained canine. This was never better illustrated than at the opening of the Sydney Opera House in 1973.

As Chairman of the Opening Committee, I was charged with the overall responsibility for the arrangements to mark the official opening by the Queen.

Following normal procedure, a handsome visitors' book was placed on a pedestal in the foyer of the building to be signed by Her Majesty and His Royal Highness The Duke of Edinburgh. To add to the atmosphere, a group of enthusiastic and patriotic volunteer women workers had arranged a magnificent bowl of flowers on a pedestal in a prominent position, which they felt would certainly attract royal notice.

Security arrangements were stringent, and on the morning of the opening sniffer dogs, accompanied by their Army handlers, scoured the vast and imposing edifice in search of possible explosives.

All went well until one Alsatian stopped at the base of the pedestal on which the flowers were placed. He sniffed, then sniffed again and squatted resolutely. The dog's Army handler immediately declared an alert and demanded that the bowl be removed and a meticulous investigation made of its contents.

Time was running out for the programme to begin. I protested, but in vain. 'This dog,' he declared, 'is one of our most reliable animals. He is never wrong.'

Despite my continued expostulations, the bowl was carried out gently to the forecourt and the flowers gingerly extracted. The search revealed nought.

What to do now? Many hours of voluntary labour had been put in by the women who had put together the magnificent display of blooms. Masculine hands made a clumsy attempt to replicate the efforts of the women volunteers. But the final result by comparison with the original was a dismal failure. It was hardly an impressive spectacle likely to attract the Queen's attention.

I demanded an explanation from the dog handler. The Army's reputation, I declared, was at stake. Somewhat lamely, he made his excuse. 'That dog came from Western Australia and it was the wildflowers from that State that he was sniffing at. That's why he stopped, and for no other reason.'

I only had one reply: 'Thank God they were not water lilies.'

Henry Kelly

Broadcaster and Journalist, Presenter Classic FM,
Presenter BBC's *Going for Gold*

I find it's always dangerous, when making an after-dinner speech, to ask people if they can hear you all right at the back. I did it once in a tough club in the north of England and a fellow well away from the top table shouted out: 'Yes . . . but I'd like to swap with somebody who can't!' Follow that!

Actually, I did manage to follow it that night with this story. It's my favourite Irish story of all time and involves the Irishman who got to the finals of *Mastermind* where Magnus Magnusson asked him what his chosen specialist subject was to be.

'The Dublin Easter Rising of 1916, please,' he said.

'Fair enough,' said Magnus, and added: 'Your time starts now:

'In what city did the Dublin Rising take place?'

'Pass.'

'In what year did the Rising take place?'

'Pass.'

'At what time of the year did the Rising take place?'

'Pass.'

At this, a woman in the audience let out a shout: 'That's the stuff, Sean,' she said, 'don't tell him anything!'

Ludovic Kennedy
Writer and Broadcaster

At the turn of the century a farmer's Irish advocate, called Sergeant Sullivan, was appearing in London before a very pompous judge. His client was a labourer from Connemara.

'Does your client,' asked the pompous judge, 'fully understand the *res ipso loquitur*?'

Sergeant Sullivan drew himself to his full height and said:

'My Lord, where my client comes from in the far west of Ireland, when the long evenings draw in and the peat fires are lit, the *res ipso loquitur* is practically the sole topic of conversation.'

*   *   *

An Irishman, who heard that the streets of London were paved with gold, came over to try his luck. He got no sleep on the boat and had to stand in the train. On leaving Euston Station, he found a five pound note lying on the pavement. He bent down to pick it up, then thought better of it. 'Hell, no,' he said to himself. 'I'm tired. I'll start properly in the morning.'

*   *   *

Both stories require an Irish accent.

Prue Leith

O.B.E.

Cook, Journalist and Author

A TV executive in a new job finds three numbered
envelopes on his desk, left by his predecessor, with
instructions to open them in order when he hits
problems.

Everything goes fine at first, then the TV ratings begin
to fall and he opens envelope No. 1. Inside is a note:
'Blame me.' So he blames his predecessor and the
pressure from the Board recedes. But after a few months
things are bad again, and he opens envelope No. 2. The
note says: 'Fire someone.' So he fires the commissioning
editor and again the heavy breathing from upstairs
diminishes.

But the ratings continue to plunge. He opens envelope
No. 3. Inside is a note: 'Prepare three envelopes.'

Viscount Leverhulme

K.G., T.D., K.St.J.
Philanthropist

A Jewish lady's husband died. She rang the local
newspaper and asked them to put a notice in the paper,
saying: 'Cohen dead.'

The newspaper told her that the minimum insertion
must have five words. 'In that case,' she said, 'put in
'Cohen dead. Volvo for sale'.'

Christopher Logue
Author, Journalist and Playwright

One summer I awoke at about three in the morning to the sound of torrential rain, mixed with that of water pouring into the kitchen of my small room.

Quick as a flash, I was out of bed, across the flat part of the roof and down the long slope of slates on the far side, soaking wet and stark naked, but able to free the back gutter of leaves and hear the water gurgle away.

But then I found I could not climb back up the slates. The downpour remained torrential. The end-bricks gave me no grip. Seeing a lighted window in one of the houses that backed on to mine, I shouted – and I have quite a loud voice – for help. A woman looked out and, instantly, put out her light. After about ten minutes I heard the voice of the lady I was living with shout over the roof from the bedroom terrace: 'Are you all right?' 'No.' 'There is a woman on the phone who says there is a naked maniac on our roof.' 'That's me.' 'Oh.' 'Get a rope or something and throw it over.'

After five minutes of miserable cold, Patricia called out: 'There is no rope in the house. Only a piece of string.' In the end my neighbour, Terry, came over the top with his wife's clothesline and I was guided back to safety.

The Rt. Hon. The Earl of Longford

K.G.

Politician and Author

Harold Macmillan, aged 90, was speaking at a small dinner at St Benet's Hall, Oxford: 'It was on just such an evening as this that I spent my first night away from home. I was a new boy at a preparatory school in Oxford, not far from here, called . . . (he paused as though forgetting the name, but he knew that it would be forthcoming) . . . 'Summerfields'. I was crying myself to sleep, but a boy in the next bed, Evelyn Baring (a typical Macmillan touch, taking us into intimacy) leant across and said, 'Don't cry, little boy. Your position is bad, but not hopeless.'

The statesman then took over. 'And so it is,' he intoned, 'in Britain today. Our position is bad, but as I look to the future I am rejuvenated with hope.'

Elizabeth Longford

C.B.E.

Royal Biographer and Author

A mother and daughter have chosen the same career, writing. How nice, we think. And there are extra advantages that no-one has ever thought of. My daughter, Antonia Fraser, writes historical biographies. So do I. One day Antonia, about to deliver a literary lecture on her latest book, was suddenly aware of her enthusiastic chairwoman concluding her introduction of the speaker with the following words:

'Antonia Fraser, as we all know, sometimes writes under the name of Elizabeth Longford.'

I am often tempted, when I feel my own latest biography needs a bit of a boost, to get the chair to introduce me in reverse:

'. . . Elizabeth Longford, as not many of you know, sometimes writes under the name of Antonia Fraser.'

In fact, there is no end to the advantageous ways in which that principle might be extended.

'And very occasionally (remember I am letting you into a publishing secret!) both Antonia and Elizabeth publish under the names of Catherine Cookson, Sue Townsend, Shirley Conran, Jane Austen – Sorry! I meant to say Jane Gardam . . .'

Lord Mackay of Ardbrecknish

Chairman, Sea Fish Industry Authority, 1990–

Two men who play a regular game of golf every
Thursday, usually on different courses, are playing
round a beautifully wooded course when they run into
two ladies playing ahead and doing so rather slowly.
After two or three holes, one of the golfers decides to go
forward and ask if they can play through.

He goes forward, disappears round the dogleg behind
trees and bushes and returns a few minutes later.

'Can we play through?' asks his companion.

'No! I never asked them. As I got closer to them, I
realised it was my wife and my mistress!'

'In that case,' says his friend, 'I'll go and ask.'

He disappear round the dogleg. On his return his
friend asks, 'Can we play through?'

'No!'

'Didn't you ask?'

'No! You know, it's a small world!'

*   *   *

Someone drops a £10 note on the street.

A rich lawyer, a poor lawyer and Santa Claus pass by.
Who picks up the £10 note?

The rich lawyer, of course. The other two are figments
of the imagination.

Francis Matthews
Actor, Radio and Television Broadcaster

I cannot hope to compete with the Robin Days and
Jeffrey Archers of the circuit. Being an actor, I have to
rely on other people's words . . . which is what I shall do
now . . .

Meeting Noel Coward towards the end of his life, Beryl
Reid commiserated with him about their mutually
declining years. 'We're both fading away,' she said. 'Oh,
it's terrible, Noel. In no time at all we'll both be pushing
up daisies. It's so depressing.'

'Nonsense, Beryl dear, you must not despair,' said
Noel. 'Remember that after you die, bits of you go on
growing. Your fingernails go on growing. The hair on
your chest goes on growing . . .'

Beryl interrupted indignantly. 'Not the hair on *my*
chest, dear!!'

'Oh Beryl darling,' scolded Noel, 'you give up hope so
easily!'

Norris McWhirter

C.B.E., M.A.

Author, Broadcaster and Publisher of the *Guinness Book of Records*

Just before the War, a doctor in London's suburbs was awakened in the small hours by an urgent Scottish accent on the telephone: 'Doctor, Doctor, there has been a calamity. My bairn has swallowed one of those silver thrippeny pieces.'

Knowing how small these little coins used to be, the doctor sleepily enquired: 'How old is it?'

Quick as a flash, back came the rasping voice: 'Nineteen nineteen.'

Cliff Michelmore

C.B.E.

Television Broadcaster and Producer, Writer

Yesterday, I had a letter from my nephew, saying: 'Dear Cliff, I am sorry it has taken me so long to thank you for my Christmas present. It would serve me right if you forgot my birthday, which is next Tuesday.'

The Hon. Sir Peter Millett
(The Hon. Mr Justice Millett)

There was once a Queen's Counsel who specialised in divorce cases. On his appointment to the Circuit Bench, he continued to spend most of his time hearing family disputes. Occasionally, however, he had to try criminal cases. One day he was trying a rape case. It was excessively boring, and he nodded off during the long afternoon. Suddenly coming round, he forgot where he was. Addressing prosecuting counsel, he inquired: 'Is there really no possibility of these two young people getting together again?'

*   *   *

A young priest, newly ordained, arrived to take up his first post. To his alarm, he was told that on his first Sunday the vicar had an engagement elsewhere, and he would have to preach the sermon. With great trepidation, he entered the pulpit, eyed the congregation and decided to confess his own inadequacy. 'Dearly beloved,' he told his listeners. 'I shall speak to you the words which Almighty God shall choose to place in my mouth. But next Sunday the good vicar will be back with something more worthy of your attention.'

*   *   *

Two Irishmen were talking in the bar.
'Have you visited the new brothel yet?'
'No.'
'Well you should. It's marvellous. You can stay all night, drink as much as you like, and there's no charge.'
'Don't be so ridiculous. I don't believe it.'
'It's true. What's more, you can have as much sex as you like, and there's no charge.'
'Go on with you. You're pulling my leg.'

'No, honestly. What's more, in the morning when you leave, they give you a £5 note.'
'Get away with you.'
'It's true, honest.'
'Have you been yourself, then?'
'No, but the wife has.'

Patrick Moore

C.B.E., F.R.A.S.

Astronomer, Broadcaster and Author

It had been a noisy stag party and the hotel manager was incensed, particularly when notified of a small fire in the bedroom of one of the guests. In the morning, the manager and the guest met face to face, and the manager went into action: 'Last night you were drunk and set fire to your bed because you were smoking!'

Luckily, the guest had the complete answer:

1. He wasn't drunk.
2. He didn't smoke.
3. The bed was already on fire by the time he got into it.

Sir Claus Moser

K.C.B., C.B.E., F.B.A.

Warden of Wadham College, Oxford, 1984–1993
Chancellor of the University of Keele, 1986–

A good starter is to say one will make a brief speech:
    'As Henry VIII said to his wives: 'I won't keep you
long'.'

Dame Merle Park

D.B.E.

Principal, Royal Ballet
Director of The Royal Ballet School, 1983–

In the village forge, the blacksmith, his striker and the
young apprentice were forging a rather tricky piece of
wrought iron. To make sure the striker brought his
hammer into action just at the right time, the blacksmith
said:

'When I get this just right, I'll nod my head and you hit
it.'

At the blacksmith's signal, the striker misjudged the
blow and caught the blacksmith a solid crack on the
head. In a towering rage the smith cursed the striker and
flung the hot metal he was holding out of the window. A
second later, the striker, equally incensed, flung his
fourteen pound hammer after the piece of wrought iron.
The young apprentice, looking from smith to striker,
wrenched the two hundred pound anvil from its block
and hurled that outside also.

Dumbfounded, both smith and striker roared at the
boy:

'What did you do that for?'

'Oh,' said the lad, 'I thought we were going to work
outside!'

*   *   *

The taciturn and forthright hillbilly, newly married that
morning, was driving his new bride back to their log
cabin. At a river crossing, the mule between the shafts
faltered. The farmer got off the cart, went to the mule's
head and, pointing a finger at the animal, said:

'That's once!'

A little later, the animal again stopped in its tracks,
refusing to cross a fallen branch. Again the driver
descended and said to the mule:

'That's twice!'

Continuing down the road, the mule once again stopped for no accountable reason and, once again, the hillbilly climbed down – but this time he took his gun and shot the animal between the eyes, and down it fell.

On seeing this, the new bride started a tirade of recriminations and abuse, accusing her new spouse of stupidity and any other accusations she could think of. The husband stood silent until the torrent of abuse ended. Then, going up to his wife, he pointed his finger at her and said:

'That's once!'

*   *   *

A genial but very drunken reveller was making erratic progress up the Strand late at night. As he weaved from side to side, a policeman went up to him and said:

'Can I help you, Sir?'

'Yes,' answered the drunk. 'Can you tell me where I can find Alcoholics Anonymash?'

'Certainly, come along with me, Sir,' offered the policeman. 'Are you going to join?'

'No!' answered the drunk, 'I'm going to reshign!'

Kathleen Peyton
Writer

I was visiting a Creative Writing Group in a small country town to give a talk, being a 'local author'. I gave my spiel in the building used for evening classes and further education, and when I had finished I turned to one old dear sitting close to me and said to her, rather patronisingly: 'And what made you come to the Creative Writing class?'

She replied, 'Because Upholstery was full, dear.'

Professor Lord Porter of Luddenham
O.M., F.R.S.
Scientist and Writer

The English must now have a visa to enter Australia.
One English visitor, having shown his passport and visa,
was then asked a long string of questions, the last of
which was: 'Do you have a criminal record?'

He apologised for the omission, saying that he had
thought this was no longer necessary.

*   *   *

A student who had attended only one lecture in a long
course subsequently sat the examination and obtained a
mark of 95%. When his astounded tutor asked him to
explain this, he replied: 'Well, Sir, I had hoped to get
100%, but the lecture confused me.'

The Rt. Hon. J. Enoch Powell

M.B.E.

Politician and Writer

I visited New Zealand from Australia in the late 1930s, when the exchange rate between Australian and New Zealand currency was more advantageous on the black market than officially. While at lunch in the Wellington Club, I enquired of my neighbour, a courtly and courteous gentleman, where I should do best purchasing New Zealand pounds, and was astonished to be cold-shouldered by him from that point onwards.

'Whom was I sitting by there?' I enquired.

'Oh,' was the answer, 'that is the Governor of the Bank of New Zealand!'

The Rt. Hon. Lord Prior

Chairman, The General Electric Company plc, 1984–
Politician

A Minister of State got the answers to two questions the wrong way round, with the following results:

'Is the Minister aware of the extensive damage done by rabbits, and will he take vigorous measures to have them eliminated?'

'No, Sir. I believe that they are rendering valuable service to farmers and that their activities should be welcomed and encouraged.'

'May I direct the attention of the Minister to the increase in the number of Inspectors and other department officials, and urge him to check their multiplication?'

'I am fully aware of the damage done by these pests, which are breeding at an alarming rate, and farmers are constantly being urged to exterminate them. Sporadic shooting is ineffectual and organised drives should be arranged at frequent intervals. It must, however, be remembered that they add variety to the countryman's diet, and that their fur has a certain market value.'

The Rt. Hon. Malcolm Rifkind

Q.C., M.P.

Secretary of State for Defence, 1992–

During the Gulf War, it was reported that if one visited the village of Crook of Devon in Kinross, in south-east Scotland, it could be seen that on the village sign someone had written under 'Crook of Devon': 'Twinned with the thief of Baghdad'!

Jancis Robinson
Wine Writer and Broadcaster

A true story

A friend of a friend of ours is a doctor who, in his spare time, writes occasionally about wine for *The Cork Examiner* in Eire.

During a visit to Champagne, he was received royally by one of the large champagne houses who assigned him his own public relations functionary. During the morning he was shown all over the vineyards and cellars and given a fascinating tasting. The PR person then took him out to an excellent lunch.

Towards the end of the meal, the PR person leaned across the table and said, 'Now, tell me about the publication you write for. Is it really about nothing but corks?'

Robert Robinson
Writer and Broadcaster

A lobster wanted to marry a crab, but her mother disapproved. 'My dear, they're so common. They don't have any money and, moreover, they walk *sideways!*'

'Just meet him, Mother,' said the lobster. She later turned up with the crab, who shook hands politely and walked in an absolutely straight line to the drawing-room.

'But I thought crabs always walked sideways!' exclaimed the mother.

'They do,' replied the crab. 'But I'm drunk.'

The Rt. Hon. Dame Angela Rumbold

D.B.E., M.P.

Politician, Deputy Chairman of the Conservative Party

A missionary was walking through the jungle completely lost, when suddenly he came across a lion. He was very frightened about this, of course, and because he was a devout Christian he thought that the only possible thing he could do was to kneel down and say his prayers. So he knelt down and started to say his prayers. This went on for a little while and nothing happened. He looked out of the corner of his eye and saw, to his great surprise, that the lion was also kneeling down in front of him, obviously saying his prayers. So he went on a little bit longer and saw that the lion was still there praying. After a few minutes he thought that maybe this lion was a Christian too, so he said to the lion, 'Very good to see you. Are you a Christian?' The lion replied, 'Oh yes, I have always been a Christian, and that is why I am saying grace before I eat you!'

Sir Harry Secombe

C.B.E.

Actor, Comedian and Singer

A good opening gag if one is wearing a dinner jacket is to say: 'When I was dressing to come here tonight, my grandson said, 'Do you have to wear that suit tonight, grandad? You know it always gives you a headache in the morning'!!!'

Constance Shacklock

O.B.E., L.R.A.M., F.R.A.M.

International Opera and Concert Singer

Quite recently, a young singing student of mine was discussing with me a harpist who played at my concert for the Kingston Arts Festival. She said, 'He looks so very young.' I replied, 'His looks are deceptive, because he's played in the Covent Garden orchestra for 20 years.'

Her reply was, 'You needn't talk, you're well pickled.' I retorted 'I hope you mean well preserved!'

*   *   *

This happened a long time ago. My husband and I were on the train, travelling to Devon for a holiday with friends. We went into the dining car for coffee, and I noticed a little lady opposite who never took her eyes off us. When we were leaving the dining car, she put her arm out and held me back. 'Can I ask you a question, luv? Are you on your honeymoon? – he's very attentive.'

I replied, 'He always is, and I've been married for over 10 years.' There was a long sigh from the lady. 'Then *you* must have the money, luv.'

I shall never forget my dear husband's face.

Ned Sherrin
Film, Theatre and Television Producer
Presenter, Director and Writer

This is a story that has to be set up as being discovered in an aunt's ancient diary. She is recording an event years earlier, when she was an attractive young girl on a Mediterranean cruise on an Italian ship.

On the first night, the Captain falls madly in love with her – as she records in her diary. On the second night, the entry reads: 'The Captain declared his love and escorted me to my cabin – I closed the door just in time.' On the third night, 'The Captain proposed marriage to me and accompanied me to my cabin – I closed the door just in time.' On the fourth night, 'The Captain escorted me to my cabin and said that if I did not let him in, he would sink the ship and drown the 500 passengers and 200-strong crew. Tonight I saved 700 people!'

Sir Neil Shields

M.C.

Chairman of the Commission for New Towns

In Papua New Guinea, there was a special dinner to
mark the end of the Chairman of the Club's year of
office.

During the course of the meal, one man turned to his
neighbour and said, 'You know, I don't really like the
Chairman.'

'Really?' said his neighbour. 'In that case, why don't
you just eat the vegetables?'

The Rt. Hon. Sir David Steel

K.B.E., M.P.

Former Leader of the Liberal Party

Quasimodo decided that he had had enough of ringing bells at Notre Dame, and hired a young lad to take his place.

Obviously, some training was necessary for the job so Quasimodo demonstrated how to ring the bells. The only problem was that the large bell had its clanger missing.

'It's quite easy,' said Quasimodo. 'All you have to do is swing it and hit it with your head.' And he gave a demonstration, swung the bell and headed it. Then it was the recruit's turn.

However, when he swung the bell and headed it, the bell hit him with such a force that he fell out of the belfry and on to the pavement below (splat!).

Within minutes, the police were on the scene. One of the constables shouted up to Quasimodo. 'Do you know this boy?'

Quasimodo replied, 'No, but his face rings a bell.'

Sir Sigmund Sternberg

J.P., F.S.C.A.

Founder of the Sternberg Centre for Judaism

Mendel Klotz and Moshe Zimmerman were walking along the main street in Odessa, engaged in an animated discussion. So absorbed were they that they did not notice the two Russian Army officers approaching and, consequently, they did not get off the pavement and into the gutter, as Jews were expected to do so that their 'betters' might pass without the contamination of a possible brush of shoulders.

Immediately, the two men were arrested and brought before the magistrate. Mendel was brought into the judge's chambers first, while Moshe waited in an anteroom.

'What have you got to say for yourself?' barked the Czar's defender of law, order and the rights of man.

'Your Grace, I was so involved in an argument with my friend that I did not notice the officers,' explained the terrified Mendel. 'I apologise. It will never happen again.'

'That's no excuse,' yelled the Russian judge. 'Thirty days' hard labour.'

Mendel was escorted back to the anteroom where Moshe was anxiously waiting.'

'How d-d-did it g-go?' asked Moshe anxiously.

'We haven't a chance,' groaned Mendel. 'I received a thirty day sentence.'

Moshe was then taken before the judge.

'Alright,' rasped the judge. 'What's your excuse?'

Moshe was numb with fright and could hardly speak. 'Y-Y-Your Honour,' he began, stuttering helplessly. 'I-I-I tr-tried t-t-t . . .' Words failed him.

'Get this imbecile out of here!' shouted the judge to the bailiff. 'I have no time for half wits.'

Moshe walked into the anteroom, his face wreathed in smiles.

'What did you get?' asked Mendel.

'None – I'm f-f-free as a b-b-b-bird.'

'What do you mean you're free? How is that possible? We were both arrested on the same charges, yet I get thirty days and you go free.'

'The t-t-t-trouble with you, Mendel,' said Moshe, 'is that you-you-you don't know how to t-t-t-talk.'

Godfrey Talbot

L.V.O., O.B.E.

Author, Broadcaster, Lecturer and Journalist

Sentences which are clear and inoffensive in print can be shockingly misleading when *spoken*. As a broadcaster, I was forced to know this very well. For instance, I was once, long ago, taken to task for saying in a news bulletin (about an important message from diplomatic Paris to the then British Prime Minister, Harold Macmillan, a message which was rushed to the PM during a Parliamentary recess/holiday): 'These dismal tidings were delivered to the PM on the golf course where he was playing a round with Lady Dorothy.' The words were unexceptional had they been printed in *The Times*, but when *spoken* the sentence sounded awful (Lady Dorothy was, of course, Sir Harold's wife).

*   *   *

One day, when I was guest speaker at a women's luncheon club, my subject was 'Round the World with the Royal Family', and of course I was recalling some of the lighter and more exciting moments during my many years of travelling the world with members of the House of Windsor (as the BBC's accredited Buckingham Palace correspondent). But I imagine that my discourse was rather less exciting than the impression given by Madam Chairman in introducing me: 'Mr Talbot,' she announced, 'is going to tell us about his adventures with the Queen.' She brought the house down.

H.H. Judge Tibber
Circuit Judge

A doctor said that, as he was getting on in years, the only name he could remember on being introduced to people at a crowded party was 'Altzheimer'.

Joanna Trollope
Author

About fifteen years ago, when I was a very novice writer of historical fiction, I was in a train going to Leeds for a *Yorkshire Post* literary lunch when I noticed, to my absolute amazement and rapture, that the man sitting opposite to me was reading a novel of mine. I gazed at him adoringly, particularly as he was reading the novel with wonderful attention. I was torn between shyness and a powerful longing to say, 'I wrote that!' followed by flinging my arms round him out of sheer gratitude. Needless to say, I did neither, and simply sat, simmering with gratification until the train reached Leeds and he looked up, saw where he was, gasped and rushed from the train. I vowed I would never be so wet if such an opportunity ever arose again.

About a year later, I was in the Marble Arch branch of Marks and Spencer, who had commissioned a dozen novelists, including me, to write books for them as an experiment in selling paperback fiction. I collected, in my wire basket, all the socks and knickers I'd come in for, then added a couple of my paperbacks and took the whole lot to the cash desk. I took a deep breath. 'Actually,' I said, as the woman on the till picked up one of the books, 'I wrote that.' She paused, gave me a pitying look, and said in a voice that matched her expression. 'Oh yes, dear. And I'm the Queen of England.'

Jill Tweedie
Author, Journalist and Scriptwriter

Sitting by his mother on a bus, a small boy is staring fascinated at a very fat woman opposite. Eventually he comments loudly on her fatness. Much embarrassed, the mother reproves him and, when they get off, tells him never to make such comments again in public, but to wait until he's at home.

Two days later, the child again becomes fascinated with a man on a bus who is covered in warts. This time he pipes up in a loud, clear voice to his mother: 'We won't talk about that man now, Mummy; we'll talk about him when we get home!'

Lord Tweedsmuir

C.B.E., C.D., F.R.S.E.

My father, when he was John Buchan the writer, wrote a great many books, one of which was a detailed history of the First World War. In the book is a chapter that describes the battle of Cambrai, which was the first time that tanks were used in that war by the Allies. He records in a footnote that during an attack, a member of a tank crew put his head out of the hatch at the top of the tank, and his wig blew away. A committee was formed in the War Office to decide whether this amounted to loss of limb, loss of personal property, or loss of field equipment. I do not know what the final decision was on the point, but I know they took an awfully long time discussing it.

Dame Ninette de Valois

C.H., D.B.E.
Founder and Director of The Royal Ballet

A little boy of five was stopped by a visitor to his mother's house. She asked him, 'How old are you, little boy?'

'I am not old,' he replied, 'I am nearly new!'

Dame Anne Warburton

D.C.V.O., C.M.G.

H.M. Diplomatic Service, 1957–85
President of the Lucy Cavendish College, Cambridge

Danish guests invited to an informal weekend country
lunch were not deterred from bringing me flowers, or a
substitute. One, presenting a well-wrapped rectangular
package, said simply 'Home baked'. In the rush the
package remained unopened. A week later, hurrying out
to a local supper party, I intended for convenience to take
the elegant box of homemade biscuits to my hostess. At
the last moment I thought a bottle would be more
appreciated. A narrow escape – when the package was
opened later, there was a copy of a book written by the
donor and charmingly inscribed to me!

*   *   *

In one street in a Danish town there were three tailors'
shops. The sign outside the first read 'Best tailor in the
world'. The second proclaimed 'Best tailor in the town'.
To which the third replied 'Best tailor in the street'.

*   *   *

Lord Halifax told of an evening when, as British
Ambassador to the United States, he was guest speaker
at a leading dining club in the Mid-West. He felt it had
gone well and preened himself when he overheard one
member saying to another that it had been a very fine
evening: 'Yes,' said the second, 'I haven't enjoyed such a
good steak for a very long time.'

June Whitfield

O.B.E.

Actress

Boring speaker:	'If you can't hear me at the back, there are some vacant seats at the front of the hall.'
Voice from hall:	'I can't hear you, but I'm quite happy where I am, thank you!'

✓ ✓
RAVENSWOOD
Caring about people with learning disabilities

In forty years Ravenswood has grown from a tiny residential school in Berkshire to a major independent charity working in the field of learning disability (mental handicap). Ravenswood today offers residential, day and respite care, education and training, recreation and holidays, and support for parents and families.

Ravenswood Village is now home to 178 people with learning disabilities, ranging in age from eight to 68. The Village has its own school, college of continuing education, synagogue, shop and coffee bar. Sixty residents are employed there or nearby.

Ravenswood has three residential homes, each for up to twenty people: Stanmore Cottage in Middlesex, The Haven in north London and Parry House in Essex. There is also a growing network of group homes, especially converted so that groups of up to eight people may live together in a family setting, with the highest degree of independence possible and professional support on hand.

Most of the people for whom Ravenswood cares live at home with their families, helped and supported by Ravenswood's team of professional social workers. Day services are available at the Kennedy Leigh Centre in Hendon, where classes are taught in everything from computers to literacy, from social skills to arts and crafts. Breaks for families will soon be available through respite care at Breathing Space, Ravenswood's latest project (and a joint venture with Norwood Child Care). At Buckets and Spades Lodge in Finchley, children will spend a single night, a few days or a fortnight in entirely child-orientated surroundings.

Unity-Ravenswood, the social side of the organisation, provides leisure activities and residential holidays. Unity-Ravenswood's activities – staff-intensive, well supervised and, especially, great fun – are open to *all* children aged from three to 18, regardless of ability.

Through The Deli, Ravenswood helps young people with learning disabilities who are hoping for success in the workplace. This government-approved Youth Training scheme in catering and allied trades operates at three sites around London. The Deli is a remarkable success, with 90 per cent of its trainees finding employment or going on to full-time, mainstream education.

If you would like to know more about Ravenswood, please write to:

Ravenswood
17 Highfield Road
London NW11 9DZ

Tel: (081) 905 5557
Fax: (081) 209 2618

Other Titles from Piatkus Books

If you have enjoyed *100 Favourite After-Dinner Stories from The Famous* you may be interested in other books published by Piatkus for after-dinner speakers and communicators. Titles include:

100 Best After-Dinner Stories Phyllis Shindler
Confident Conversation: How to Talk in Any Business or Social Situation Dr. Lillian Glass
My Lords, Ladies and Gentlemen: The Best and Funniest After-Dinner Stories from the Famous Phyllis Shindler
Powerspeak: The Complete Guide to Public Speaking and Communication Dorothy Leeds
Confident Speaking: How to Communicate Effectively Using the Power Talk System Christian H. Godefroy and Stephanie Barrat
Raise Your Glasses: The Best and Wittiest Anecdotes and After-Dinner Stories from the Famous Phyllis Shindler

For a free brochure with further information on our range of titles, please write to:

Piatkus Books
Freepost 7 (WD 4505)
London, W1E 4EZ